Special
Packaging

Pepin van Roojen

Pepin

Amsterdam & Singapore

Pepin® is a registered trademark of
Pepin Holding BV

ISBN 978 90 5768 159 2

Published by:
The Pepin Press BV
P.O. Box 10349
1001 EH Amsterdam, The Netherlands

+31 20 4202021
mail@pepinpress.com
www.pepinpress.com

Concept & design: Pepin van Roojen
Layout & project management: Jakob Hronek
Editorial & production supervisor: Kevin Haworth

10 9 8 7 6 5 4 3 2 1
2016 15 14 13 12 11

Manufactured in Singapore

Contents

Structural package design

Packaging design technology has made enormous advances in recent years, largely due to continuing developments in digital capabilities, both in design and manufacturing. The content in this series of books was produced using the latest technology and this series aims to bring the benefits of these technical advances to the reader. The latest 3-D drafting and testing software was used to create and develop all of the designs and the prototype templates were cut and creased using digitally-driven cutting tables. All of this means that the accuracy of the designs is guaranteed; they are functional and fully scalable. However, do keep in mind that the thickness of the material used must be taken into consideration when designing any package. Adjustments to the designs will likely to be necessary when dimensions are changed or other materials are used.

Packaging standards

Several organizations worldwide publish sets of industry standards for the design of structural packaging. The most widely used are the design code established jointly by FEFCO (European Federation of Corrugated Board Manufacturers) and ESBO (European Solid Board Organization) and the category style characteristics defined by the PPC (American Paperboard Packaging Council).

Materials

In packaging design and manufacturing, a distinction is made between the following types of fibre-based materials:

paper: material with a weight of less than 225 gsm (grams per square meter)

paperboard: solid material with a weight of more than 225 gsm

cardboard: solid material with a weight between 150 and 600 gsm; more rigid than paper and often coated

corrugated board: fluted paper glued onto or between paper or board. The most common corrugated boards are:

single face: one layer of fluted paper glued onto one layer of paper or board

double face or single wall: one layer of fluted paper glued between two layers of paper or board

double wall: two layers of fluted paper glued between three layers of paper or board

triple wall: three layers of fluted paper glued between four layers of paper or board

In addition to the material and number of layers, corrugated board is defined by the type of flute. Flute type is generally designated using a letter code and is determined by the number of flutes per linear meter (or foot) and the flute thickness.

Three types of material were used for the prototypes in this book: 350 gsm cardboard, 1 mm G-flute corrugated board, and 1.5 mm E-flute corrugated board. For the FEFCO standard designs in **Basic Packaging**, 3 mm B-flute corrugated board was simulated in the 3-D images.

Technical considerations

When creasing for folds in solid board, the crease should be on the outside of the planned fold line, i.e. the fold folds away from the crease. However, for folds in corrugated board, the crease (or score) should be on the inside of the fold.

In many cases, the direction of the grain of the material – or of the flutes in corrugated board – is important. The grain/fluting can affect the quality of a crease and the overall stability of a package. It is best to discuss this with materials suppliers and manufacturers before completing a design.

The surface of the material used is an important issue to consider when choosing the type and quality of printing and finishing. For example, rough board is not suitable for fine or high-contrast graphics, whereas high-quality paperboard or corrugated board (with at least one smooth, coated face) allows for high standards of offset printing, foil stamping, embossing, etc.

Packaging dimensions

When designing a package, the most important consideration is, of course, the dimensions of the product to be packaged. However, there are additional matters to consider, such as leaving space for protective padding or a liner, the outside dimensions of the package and how it can be stacked and/or fit onto a pallet, material waste during production, and production speed.

Package design

Like most other forms of structural design, most package design today is done using CAD (computer aided design) programs. These exist in many forms, from simple software that allows you to create basic structures, to highly advanced applications that manage complete production processes.

EskoArtwork is a world leader in the development of package design software. Their ArtiosCAD software has been used in the industry for decades. This cutting-edge program provides a complete solution for package design in a professional manufacturing environment. However, for graphic, packaging and product designers who do not need the full functionality of ArtiosCAD, EskoArtwork's software plug-ins for programs such as Adobe Illustrator® and Photoshop® are an excellent and more affordable alternative. All of the designs in this book were created using these plug-ins and a demo version of the software is included on the CD with this book.

Prototypes

Good software programs facilitate the thorough examination of designs and help reduce the need for physical testing. In EskoArtwork's Visualizer plug-in, for example, many types of graphics and special finishes can be simulated realistically. There is even the possibility of visualizing the product under different lighting conditions.

When a design is nearing its final production phase, however, it is essential that a prototype be made. Of course, this can be done by hand. But using a proof printer to print the graphics on the intended material and a digitally-driven cutting and creasing table to produce an accurate mock-up is a much better approach to generating a realistic prototype.

Cutting tables come in a variety of sizes and with a wide range of capabilities. Some models are even suitable for the output of small production runs.

Verpackungsformgebung

Die Verpackungsformgebung hat in den letzten Jahren sowohl fertigungs- als auch konstruktionstechnisch enorme Fortschritte gemacht, größtenteils dank der ständig weiter entwickelten Computertechnik. Unsere Buchreihe will den Lesern die Vorteile dieser technischen Fortschritte zugänglich machen; die Inhalte sind mit neuester Technologie erarbeitet. Alle Entwürfe wurden mit der neuesten 3-D-Design- und Testsoftware entwickelt und die Prototypen auf digital gesteuerten Schneidtischen zugeschnitten und gefalzt. Dadurch ist die Genauigkeit der Vorlagen garantiert; alle Designs funktionieren und sind voll skalierbar. Allerdings muss man beim Entwurf einer Verpackung die Materialstärke im Auge behalten. Denn variiert man die Dimensionen oder das Material, müssen meist auch die Vorlagen entsprechend angepasst werden.

Verpackungsstandards

Mehrere internationale Organisationen geben Standards zur Verpackungsformgebung für die Industrie heraus. Am verbreitetsten sind der zusammen von der FEFCO (Europäische Vereinigung der Wellpapphersteller) und der ESBO (Europäische Organisation für Vollpappe) erarbeitete Code und die vom PPC (American Paperboard Packaging Council) definierten Typenkategorien.

Materialien

Bei der Konstruktion und Fertigung von Verpackungen unterscheidet man folgende faserhaltige Materialien:

Papier: Materialien unter 225 g/m² (Gramm pro Quadratmeter)

Pappe: feste Materialien über 225 g/m²

Karton: feste Materialien zwischen 150 und 600 g/m²; steifer als Papier und oft beschichtet bzw. „gestrichen"

Wellpappe: gewelltes, zwischen Papier oder Karton geleimtes Papier. Die geläufigsten Wellpapptypen sind:

einseitige: eine Lage gewelltes Papier auf eine Lage Papier oder Karton aufgeleimt

zweiseitige oder **einwellige:** eine Lage gewelltes Papier zwischen zwei Lagen Papier oder Karton geleimt

zweiwellige oder **Duplex:** zwei Lagen gewelltes Papier zwischen drei Lagen Papier oder Karton geleimt

dreiwellige: drei Lagen gewelltes Papier zwischen vier Lagen Papier oder Karton geleimt

Außer nach Materialien und Anzahl der Lagen unterscheidet man Wellpappe auch nach Wellentypen. Wellentypen differenziert man meist nach der Anzahl der Wellen pro Meter (oder Fuß) bzw. ihrer Dicke und bezeichnet sie mit Buchstabencodes.

Für die Muster in diesem Buch haben wir drei Materialtypen verwendet: Karton mit 350 g/m², 1-mm-G-Wellen-Pappe und 1,5-mm-E-Wellen-Pappe. Für die 3-D-Grafiken der FEFCO-Standardmuster aus **Standard-Verpackungsdesigns** haben wir 3-mm-B-Wellpappe simuliert.

Technische Aspekte

Wird vor dem Falzen gerillt, muss bei festem Karton die Rillung auf der Außenseite der geplanten Falzlinie liegen, d. h. die Falz wird von der Rillung weg gebogen. Beim Falzen von Wellpappe dagegen sollte die Rille (oder Ritzung) auf der Falzinnenseite liegen.

Häufig ist die Faserlaufrichtung des Materials – bei Wellpappe die Wellenlaufrichtung – entscheidend. Die Faser- bzw. Wellenlaufrichtung kann die Qualität einer Rillung und die Stabilität der Verpackung insgesamt beeinflussen. Am besten klärt man dies noch vor Fertigstellung des Entwurfs mit dem Materialzulieferer bzw. Hersteller.

Bei der Entscheidung über Art und Qualität von Aufdrucken und Finishs ist auf jeden Fall die Oberfläche des verwendeten Materials zu berücksichtigen. So ist etwa grober Karton für detaillierte und kontrastreiche Grafiken ungeeignet, während hochwertiger Karton oder Wellpappe (mit mindestens einer glatten, gestrichenen Seite) hohe Qualität bei Offsetdruck, Prägung, Folienprägung etc. ermöglichen.

Verpackungsabmessungen

Das Wichtigste beim Entwurf einer Verpackung sind natürlich die Maße des zu verpackenden Produkts. Doch ist noch mehr zu berücksichtigen – z. B. eventueller Platzbedarf für Schutzpolster oder Zwischenfutter, die Außenmaße der Verpackung und ihre Eignung zum Verstauen bzw. Stapeln auf Paletten, die Materialabfallmenge bei der Fertigung und die Produktionsgeschwindigkeit.

Verpackungsformgebung

Wie bei Konstruktionsentwürfen üblich, werden die meisten Verpackungsdesigns heutzutage mit CAD-Programmen (CAD = computer-aided design) erstellt. Es gibt sie in allen möglichen Formen von einfacher Software für Standarddesigns bis hin zu Hightech-Anwendungen, die komplette Fertigungsabläufe verwalten.

EskoArtwork ist ein weltweit führender Entwickler von Verpackungsdesign-Software. EskoArtworks CAD-Software ArtiosCAD wird seit Jahrzehnten in der Industrie eingesetzt und bietet State-of-the-Art-Komplettlösungen für die industrielle Verpackungsentwicklung. Für Grafik-, Verpackungs- und Produktdesigner, die nicht alle Funktionen von ArtiosCAD brauchen, sind EskoArtworks Plug-Ins für Programme wie Adobe Illustrator® und Photoshop® eine perfekte – und erschwinglichere – Alternative. Alle Entwürfe in diesem Buch haben wir mit diesen Plug-Ins erstellt; eine Demoversion der Software liegt dem Buch auf CD-ROM bei.

Prototypen

Gute Software erleichtert das gründliche Über-
prüfen der Entwürfe und ersetzt einen Teil der
Praxistests. Mit EskoArtworks Visualizer-Plug-In
etwa lassen sich alle möglichen Grafiken und spe-
zielle Finishs realistisch simulieren. Man kann
damit sogar das Aussehen des Produkts unter ver-
schiedenen Lichtverhältnissen darstellen.
Ist ein Entwurf bis kurz vor Anlauf der Produktion
gediehen, muss auf jeden Fall ein Prototyp ange-
fertigt werden. Das geht natürlich auch manuell.
Ein wesentlich besseres Verfahren, realistische
Prototypen zu bekommen, ist aber ein genaues
Modell mit einem Testdrucker, der das vorgesehene
Material bedruckt, und einer digital gesteuerten
Rill- und Stanzmaschine herzustellen.
Schneid- bzw. Stanzmaschinen gibt es in verschie-
denen Größen und mit unterschiedlichsten Funk-
tionen. Einige eignen sich sogar zur Fertigung
von Kleinserien.

Modèles structuraux de conditionnement

En matière de modèles de conditionnement, la technologie a accompli de formidables avancées au cours de ces dernières années, en grande partie grâce aux progrès permanents dans le domaine numérique, à la fois en termes de conception et de fabrication. Le contenu de cette série de manuels a été conçu à l'aide des technologies les plus récentes et cette série a pour but de faire bénéficier le lecteur de ces avancées techniques. La création et le développement de tous les modèles ont été réalisés à l'aide du tout dernier logiciel de test et de dessin en 3D. Les patrons des prototypes ont été découpés et refoulés en utilisant des tables de découpe à commande numérique. Cette exigence dans le choix des outils est la garantie de modèles de précision, à la fois fonctionnels et entièrement modulables. Toutefois, n'oubliez pas que l'épaisseur du matériau utilisé doit être prise en considération lors de la conception de tout produit de conditionnement. Les modèles devront vraisemblablement être ajustés en cas de modification des dimensions ou d'utilisation d'autres matériaux.

Normes de conditionnement

À l'échelle internationale, plusieurs organisations éditent des corpus de normes industrielles relatives à la conception de conditionnements structuraux. Les plus répandues sont d'une part le code de conception établi conjointement par la FEFCO (European Federation of Corrugated Board Manufacturers) et l'ESBO (European Solid Board Organization) et d'autre part les caractéristiques des types de catégorie définies par le PPC (American Paperboard Packaging Council).

Matériaux

En matière de conception et de fabrication de produits de conditionnement, il convient de faire la distinction entre les types de matériaux à base de fibres suivants :

papier : matériau d'un grammage inférieur à 225 g/m² (grammes par mètre carré)

papier-carton : matériau solide d'un grammage supérieur à 225 g/m²

carton : matériau solide d'un grammage compris entre 150 et 600 g/m²; plus rigide que du papier et souvent couché

carton ondulé : papier cannelé collé sur ou entre du papier ou du carton. Les cartons ondulés les plus courants sont les suivants :

simple face : une couche de papier cannelé collée sur une couche de papier ou de carton

double face ou **simple cannelure :** une couche de papier cannelé collée entre deux couches de papier ou de carton

double cannelure : deux couches de papier cannelé collées entre trois couches de papier ou de carton

triple cannelure : trois couches de papier cannelé collées entre quatre couches de papier ou de carton

Outre le matériau et le nombre de couches, le carton ondulé est défini par le type de cannelure. Le type de cannelure est généralement désigné à l'aide d'une lettre-code et est déterminé par le nombre de cannelures par mètre linéaire (ou pied) et par l'épaisseur de la cannelure. Dans ce manuel, trois types de matériaux sont utilisés pour les prototypes : 350 g/m² de carton, 1 mm de carton ondulé en cannelure G et 1,5 mm de carton ondulé en cannelure E. Pour les modèles standard FEFCO du manuel **Modèles de base**, la simulation des images en 3D a été effectuée en prenant pour hypothèse 3 mm de carton ondulé en cannelure B.

Considérations techniques

Lors de l'opération de rainage visant à créer des plis dans un carton solide, le rainage doit être à l'extérieur de la ligne de pliure prévue, c'est-à-dire que le pliage se replie à partir de la pliure. Toutefois, dans le cas de pliages effectués dans du carton ondulé, la pliure (ou ligne de refoulage) doit être à l'intérieur du pli.

Dans de nombreux cas, le sens du grain du matériau – ou des cannelures dans le carton ondulé – est important. Le grain/la cannelure peut en effet affecter la qualité du refoulage et amoindrir la stabilité globale d'un conditionnement.

Il est préférable de consulter les fournisseurs et les fabricants des matériaux avant de réaliser un modèle.

La surface du matériau utilisé est un point important à prendre en considération lors de la sélection du type et de la qualité d'impression et de finition. Par exemple, un carton rêche n'est pas approprié pour des graphismes exigeant finesse et forts contrastes, alors que le papier-carton de haute qualité ou le carton ondulé (avec au moins une face couchée et lisse) permet des normes élevées d'impression offset, de dorure à la presse, de gaufrage, etc.

Dimensions de conditionnement

Lors de la conception d'un produit de conditionnement, l'aspect le plus important à prendre en considération porte, bien entendu, sur les dimensions du produit à conditionner. Toutefois, des impératifs supplémentaires doivent être considérés, comme la nécessité de laisser suffisamment d'espace pour le rembourrage de protection ou une doublure, les dimensions extérieures de l'emballage et la façon dont il peut être empilé et/ou placé sur une palette, les déchets des matériaux générés au cours de la production et la vitesse de production.

Conception de produits de conditionnement

A l'instar de la plupart des autres formes de conception structurelle, la plupart des modèles de conditionnement sont réalisés aujourd'hui à l'aide de programmes CAO (conception assistée par ordinateur - CAD en anglais). Ceux-ci existent sous de nombreuses formes : du simple logiciel qui vous permet de créer des structures de base jusqu'à des applications hautement avancées qui gèrent des processus de production complets.

EskoArtwork est un leader mondial en matière de développement de logiciel de conception de produits de conditionnement. Leur logiciel CAO « ArtiosCAD » est utilisé dans l'industrie depuis des décennies. Ce programme de pointe fournit une solution complète pour la conception de produits de conditionnement dans un environnement de fabrication professionnel. Toutefois pour des concepteurs de graphismes, de conditionnements et de produits qui n'ont pas besoin de l'intégralité des fonctionnalités d'ArtiosCAD, les plug-ins du logiciel d'EskoArtwork conçus pour des programmes tels que Adobe Illustrator® et Photoshop® constituent une excellente alternative tout en étant plus abordables. Tous les modèles de ce manuel ont été créés en utilisant ces plug-ins et une version de démonstration du logiciel est incluse sur le CD fourni avec ce manuel.

Prototypes

Les programmes logiciels de bonne qualité facilitent l'examen approfondi des modèles et aident à réduire le besoin d'essai physique. Dans le plug-in d'EskoArtwork « Visualizer », par exemple, un grand nombre de types de graphismes et de finitions spéciales peut être simulé de manière réaliste. Il existe même la possibilité de visualiser le produit sous différents éclairages.

Toutefois, lorsqu'un modèle approche de sa phase de production finale, il est essentiel de réaliser un prototype. Bien entendu, ceci peut être effectué à la main. Mais l'utilisation d'une imprimante à épreuves pour imprimer les graphismes sur le matériau souhaité et d'une table de découpe et de refoulement à commande numérique pour produire une maquette précise est une bien meilleure approche pour générer un prototype réaliste.

Les tables de découpe sont disponibles dans une grande variété de tailles et dans un large éventail de capacités. Certains modèles sont même appropriés pour la production de petits tirages.

Diseño de estructuras para embalajes

La tecnología del diseño de embalajes avanza a pasos agigantados, en buena parte gracias a las continuas innovaciones digitales en los ámbitos del diseño y la producción. El contenido de esta colección se ha creado con la tecnología más reciente para hacer llegar las ventajas de estos avances técnicos al lector. Cada uno de los diseños se ha concebido y desarrollado con el *software* de dibujo en 3D y de pruebas más innovador, y los prototipos se han cortado y hendido con mesas de corte digitales. Estos aspectos garantizan la precisión de los diseños, todos ellos funcionales y de escala modificable. No obstante, a la hora de diseñar un embalaje hay que tener en cuenta el grosor del material. Si se cambian las dimensiones o se utilizan materiales distintos puede que sea preciso ajustar las plantillas.

Estándares para el embalaje

Algunas organizaciones internacionales publican una serie de estándares para el diseño de estructuras para embalajes. El principal referente es el código de diseño concebido por la FEFCO (Federación Europea de Fabricantes de Cartón Ondulado) y la ESBO (Organización Europea de Cartón Sólido), así como las características estilísticas por categorías definidas por el PPC (Consejo para Embalajes de Cartón norteamericano).

Materiales

En los ámbitos del diseño y la fabricación de embalajes se distingue entre los siguientes tipos de materiales de fibra:

papel: material con un gramaje inferior a 225 g/m2

cartulina: material sólido con un gramaje superior a 225 g/m2

cartón: material sólido con un gramaje de 150 a 600 g/m2, más rígido que el papel y a menudo tratado

cartón ondulado: papel ondulado pegado sobre una o dos hojas de papel o de cartón. Los cartones ondulados más habituales son:

de simple cara: una capa de papel ondulado pegada sobre una capa de papel o de cartón

de doble cara: una capa de papel ondulado pegada entre dos capas de papel o de cartón

de doble-doble cara: dos capas de papel ondulado pegadas entre tres capas de papel o de cartón

de triple cara: tres capas de papel ondulado pegadas entre cuatro capas de papel o de cartón

El cartón ondulado no solo depende del material y la cantidad de capas, sino también del tipo de onda. Esta tipología varía en función de la cantidad de ondas por metro lineal y del grosor, y suele indicarse mediante letras.

Para los prototipos de este libro se han utilizado tres tipos de material: cartón de 350 g/m2, cartón ondulado onda G de 1 mm y cartón ondulado onda E de 1,5 mm. En el caso de los diseños estándar de la FEFCO de **Diseños básicos**, las imágenes en 3D se simularon con cartón ondulado onda B de 3 mm.

Aspectos técnicos

Al doblar cartón sólido, el pliegue debe quedar por fuera de la línea o, dicho de otro modo, el doblez debe realizarse hacia el exterior. Por el contrario, al doblar cartón ondulado el doblez debe realizarse hacia el interior.

También hay que tener en cuenta la dirección del grano del material o, en el caso del cartón ondulado, de las ondas. El grano o las ondas pueden afectar a la calidad del pliegue y a la estabilidad del embalaje. Antes de acometer un diseño se recomienda consultar con el fabricante y el proveedor del material.

Para poder elegir el tipo y la calidad de la impresión y el acabado es necesario valorar la superficie del material. Por ejemplo, el cartón sin tratar no es apto para los gráficos definidos o con mucho contraste, mientras que el cartón sólido u ondulado de alta calidad (con una cara lisa tratada como mínimo) permite aplicar las técnicas más avanzadas de impresión en *offset*, estampado en caliente o gofrado, entre otras.

Dimensiones del embalaje

Lógicamente, lo más importante a la hora de diseñar un embalaje es tener en cuenta las dimensiones del producto. Aun así, hay otros aspectos que merecen atención, como el espacio para el acolchado de protección o el revestimiento, las dimensiones externas del embalaje y la forma de apilarlo y/o almacenarlo en un palé, la merma de material en la fase de producción y la velocidad de la cadena de montaje.

Diseño del embalaje

Como muchos otros diseños, hoy en día los embalajes suelen crearse con programas de diseño asistido por ordenador (CAD). Existen todo tipo de versiones, desde sencillas aplicaciones de *software* que permiten crear estructuras básicas, hasta programas de última generación que gestionan todo el proceso de producción.

EskoArtwork es uno de los principales desarrolladores de *software* para el diseño de embalaje. Su aplicación ArtiosCAD se utiliza en el sector desde hace décadas. Esta tecnología punta ofrece una solución integral para diseñar embalajes en un entorno profesional. Los diseñadores gráficos, de embalajes y de productos que no requieren todas las prestaciones de ArtiosCAD encontrarán una alternativa excelente y asequible en los *plug-ins* de EskoArtwork para programas como Adobe Illustrator® y Photoshop®. Todos los diseños de este volumen se han creado con estos *plug-ins*, que se incluyen en formato de versión de prueba en el CD adjunto.

Prototipos

Un buen programa de *software* debe facilitar la
supervisión de los diseños y limitar la necesidad
de realizar pruebas físicas. El *plug-in* Visualizer de EskoArtwork, por ejemplo, permite simular
varios tipos de gráficos y acabados especiales
con mucho realismo. Incluso existe la posibilidad
de visualizar el producto con distintos tipos de
iluminación.

Dicho esto, cuando un diseño entra en la fase de
producción final resulta imprescindible fabricar
un prototipo. Si bien puede hacerse a mano, lo
más aconsejable es imprimir los gráficos sobre el
material elegido con una impresora de prueba y a
continuación procesarlos a través de una mesa de
corte y hendido para generar una maqueta exacta
del diseño.

En el mercado existen mesas de corte de todos
los tamaños y prestaciones. Algunos modelos
incluso están preparados para producir pequeñas
tiradas.

Progettazione strutturale di imballaggi

La tecnologia di progettazione degli imballaggi ha fatto dei progressi enormi negli ultimi anni, specialmente grazie ai continui sviluppi delle capacità digitali di progettazione e produzione. Il contenuto di questa serie di libri è stato prodotto utilizzando le tecnologie più recenti e mira ad offrire al lettore i vantaggi di questi progressi tecnologici. Per creare e sviluppare tutti i progetti è stato utilizzato il più recente software di creazione di bozze e testing 3-D, mentre i modelli dei prototipi sono stati tagliati e piegati utilizzando tabelle di taglio impostate in modo digitale. Tutto ciò significa che viene garantita la precisione dei progetti, i quali sono pienamente funzionali e scalabili. Tuttavia, è importante ricordare che in fase di progettazione dell'imballaggio è necessario tenere conto anche dello spessore del materiale utilizzato, ed è inoltre possibile che siano necessarie modifiche ai disegni quando si cambiano le dimensioni o si utilizzano altri materiali.

Standard di imballaggio

Diverse organizzazioni di tutto il mondo pubblicano una serie di standard industriali per la progettazione di imballaggi strutturali. Gli standard utilizzati in modo più diffuso sono rappresentati dal codice di progettazione stabilito in modo congiunto dalla FEFCO (Federazione europea dei fabbricanti di cartone ondulato) e dalla ESBO (Organizzazione europea del cartone solido), oltre che dalle caratteristiche di stile di categoria definite dalla PPC (Consiglio americano per gli imballaggi in cartonato).

Materiali

Nella progettazione e produzione degli imballaggi, si distinguono i seguenti tipi di materiali basati su fibre:

Carta: materiale con peso inferiore a 225 gsm (grammi per metro quadro)

Cartonato: materiale solido con un peso superiore a 225 gsm

Cartone: Materiale solido con un peso tra 150 e 600 gsm, più rigido della carta e spesso ricoperto

Cartone ondulato: carta scanalata incollata su o tra carta o cartone. I cartoni ondulati più comuni sono:

lato singolo: uno strato di carta scanalata incollato con uno strato di carta o cartone

lato doppio o **parete singola:** uno strato di carta scanalata incollato tra due strati di carta o cartone

parete doppia: due strati di carta scanalata incollati tra tre strati di carta o cartone

parete tripla: tre strati di carta scanalata incollati tra quattro strati di carta o cartone

Oltre che dal materiale e dal numero di strati, il cartone ondulato viene definito dal tipo di scanalatura. Il tipo di scanalatura viene in genere progettato utilizzando un codice alfabetico e viene determinato dal numero di scanalature per metro (o piede) lineare, oltre che dallo spessore della scanalatura.

Per i prototipi di questo libro sono stati utilizzati tre tipi di materiale: cartone da 350 gsm, cartone ondulato con scanalatura a G da 1 mm e cartone ondulato con scanalatura ad E da 1,5 mm. Per i disegni dello standard FEFCO in **Imballaggi di base**, il cartone ondulato con scanalatura a B da 3 mm è stato simulato nelle immagini in 3-D.

Considerazioni tecniche

Quando si effettuano piegature con materiale di cartone solido, la piega deve trovarsi all'esterno della riga di piegatura pianificata, ovvero la piegatura si svolge sviluppandosi dalla piega. Tuttavia, per le piegature con il cartone ondulato, la piega (o rigatura) deve trovarsi all'interno della piegatura.

In molti casi è importante la direzione della venatura del materiale o delle scanalature del cartone ondulato. La venatura/scanalatura può influire sulla qualità della piega e la stabilità complessiva di un imballaggio. Prima di completare un disegno, è pertanto preferibile discutere con i fornitori e i produttori dei materiali.

La superficie del materiale utilizzato è un problema importante da prendere in considerazione in fase di scelta del tipo e della qualità della stampa e della finitura. Ad esempio, il cartone grezzo non è adatto a grafica fine o ad alto contrasto, mentre il cartonato o il cartone ondulato di alta qualità (che abbia almeno un lato liscio e ricoperto) permette alti standard di stampa in offset, stampa di lamine, impressione a secco ecc.

Dimensioni degli imballaggi

Quando viene progettato un imballaggio, la considerazione più importante riguarda ovviamente le dimensioni del prodotto da imballare. Tuttavia, è necessario prendere in considerazione altri aspetti, ad esempio lo spazio da lasciare per il materiale protettivo per l'imbottitura o un'eventuale calotta interna, le dimensioni esterne dell'imballaggio e le modalità con cui questo verrà accatastato e/o inserito in un pallet, oltre al materiale di scarto durante la produzione e la velocità di produzione.

Progettazione dell'imballaggio

Allo stesso modo di altre forme di disegno strutturale, la maggior parte delle progettazioni degli imballaggi viene oggi effettuata utilizzando programmi CAD. Questi sono disponibili in diverse forme, da semplice software che consente di creare strutture di base, fino ad applicazioni altamente avanzate che gestiscono processi di produzione completi.

EskoArtwork è un'azienda leader mondiale nello sviluppo di software per la progettazione di imballaggi. Il software ArtiosCAD di questa società è stato utilizzato nel settore per decenni, dato che questo programma d'avanguardia offre una soluzione completa per la progettazione di imballaggi in ambienti di produzione professionali. Tuttavia, per i progettisti grafici, di imballaggi e di prodotti che non necessitano della piena funzionalità del software ArtiosCAD, i plug-in software di EskoArtwork per programmi quali Adobe Illustrator® e Photoshop® rappresentano un'alternativa eccellente e più economica. Tutti i progetti di questo libro sono stati creati utilizzando questi plug-in, mente una versione demo del software è inclusa nel CD fornito con questo libro.

Prototipi

Programmi software progettati in modo ottimale consentono un attento esame dei progetti e aiutano a ridurre la necessità di test fisici. Ad esempio, con il plug-in Visualizer di EskoArtwork è possibile simulare realisticamente diversi tipi di grafica e finiture speciali. Esiste anche la possibilità di visualizzare il prodotto in diverse condizioni di luce.

Tuttavia, quando un progetto si approssima alla propria fase di produzione finale, è essenziale creare un prototipo. Ovviamente questa operazione può essere effettuata a mano, ma l'uso di una stampante per bozze per stampare la grafica sul materiale di destinazione, oltre a una tabella di taglio e piega impostata in modo digitale per produrre un menabò preciso, rappresenta un approccio decisamente migliore per la creazione di un prototipo realistico.
Le tabelle di taglio vengono fornite in diversi formati e con un'ampia gamma di possibilità, mentre alcuni modelli sono adatti anche alle piccole produzioni.

Desenho de estruturas para embalagens

A tecnologia do desenho de embalagens revelou avanços notáveis nos últimos anos, em grande parte devido ao desenvolvimento das capacidades digitais, tanto ao nível do desenho como da produção. O conteúdo desta série de livros foi produzido utilizando as mais recentes tecnologias e tem como objectivo dar a conhecer as vantagens destes avanços tecnológicos ao leitor. Foi utilizado o *software* de desenho e teste em 3D mais avançado para criar e desenvolver todos os desenhos e os modelos do protótipo foram cortados e vincados utilizando mesas de corte digitais. Tudo isto significa que os desenhos são garantidamente precisos, funcionais e completamente escalonáveis. No entanto, tenha em atenção que a espessura do material utilizado deve ser tida em consideração quando se desenha uma embalagem. Provavelmente será necessário ajustar os desenhos quando são alteradas as dimensões ou os materiais utilizados.

Padrões de embalagem

Várias organizações em todo o mundo publicam conjuntos de normas industriais para o desenho de estruturas para embalagens. O mais utilizado é o código de desenho estabelecido conjuntamente entre a FEFCO (Federação Europeia dos Fabricantes de Cartão Canelado) e a ESBO (Organização Europeia de Cartão Compacto) e as características de estilo da categoria definidas pelo PPC (Conselho Americano para Embalagens de Cartão).

Materiais

No desenho e produção de embalagens, é feita uma distinção entre os seguintes tipos de materiais à base de fibras:

papel: material com um peso inferior a 225 g/m2 (gramas por metro quadrado)

cartão: material sólido com um peso superior a 225 g/m2

papelão: material sólido com um peso entre 150 e 600 g/m2; mais rígido do que o papel e muitas vezes revestido

cartão canelado: papel canelado colado a ou entre papel ou cartão. Os tipos de cartão canelado mais comuns são:

face simples: uma camada de papel canelado colada a uma camada de papel ou cartão

face dupla ou **parede simples:** uma camada de papel canelado colada entre duas camadas de papel ou cartão

parede dupla: duas camadas de papel canelado coladas entre três camadas de papel ou cartão

parede tripla: três camadas de papel canelado coladas entre quatro camadas de papel ou cartão

Além do material e do número de camadas, o cartão canelado é definido pelo tipo de canelura. O tipo de canelura é normalmente designado utilizando um código de letras e é determinado pelo número de caneluras por metro linear (ou pé) e pela sua espessura.

Foram utilizados três tipos de material para os protótipos presentes neste livro: papelão de 350 gm2, cartão canelado de canelura G com 1 mm e cartão canelado de canelura E com 1,5 mm. Para os desenhos-padrão da FEFCO em **Desenhos Básicos**, foi simulado em 3D um cartão canelado de canelura B com 3 mm.

Considerações técnicas

Ao aplicar os vincos para dobra em cartão sólido, o vinco deverá estar na parte exterior da linha de dobra pretendida, ou seja, a dobra é efectuada no lado oposto ao vinco. No entanto, no caso das dobras em cartão canelado, o vinco (ou corte) deverá estar no lado interior da dobra.

Em muitos casos, a direcção do grão do material – ou da canelura no caso do cartão canelado – é importante. O grão/canelura pode afectar a qualidade do vinco e a estabilidade geral da embalagem. É aconselhável discutir este aspecto com os fornecedores e fabricantes de materiais antes de completar um desenho.

A superfície do material utilizado é um aspecto importante a considerar na escolha do tipo e qualidade da impressão e acabamento. Por exemplo, o cartão áspero não é adequado para gráficos delicados ou de alto contraste, enquanto o cartão ou cartão canelado de alta qualidade (com, pelo menos, uma face suave e revestida) permite altos padrões de impressão em *offset*, estampagem com película metalizada, relevos, etc.

Dimensões das embalagens

Ao desenhar uma embalagem, a consideração mais importante é, sem dúvida, as dimensões do produto embalado. No entanto, existem outros aspectos a considerar, tais como deixar espaço adicional para enchimento de protecção ou v, as dimensões exteriores da embalagem e como pode ser empilhada e/ou acomodada numa palete, os resíduos de materiais durante a produção e a velocidade de produção.

Desenho de embalagens

Tal como a maioria dos outros tipos de desenho de estruturas, grande parte do desenho de embalagens hoje em dia é feito utilizando programas CAD (desenho assistido por computador). Existe uma grande variedade de programas, desde um *software* simples que lhe permite criar estruturas básicas, a aplicações altamente avançadas que gerem todo o processo de produção.

A EskoArtwork é líder mundial no desenvolvimento de *software* para desenho de embalagens. O seu *software* ArtiosCAD tem sido usado no sector há décadas. Este avançado programa oferece uma solução completa para desenho de embalagens num ambiente de produção profissional. No entanto, para os *designers* gráficos, de embalagens e de produtos que não necessitam de todas as funcionalidades do ArtiosCAD, os *plug-ins* de software EskoArtwork para programas como Adobe Illustrator® e Photoshop® são uma excelente alternativa económica. Todos os desenhos presentes neste livro foram criados utilizando estes *plug-ins* e está incluída uma versão de avaliação do *software* no CD que acompanha o livro.

Protótipos

Os bons programas de *software* facilitam uma avaliação exaustiva dos desenhos e ajudam a reduzir a necessidade de testes físicos. No *plug-in* Visualizer da EskoArtwork, por exemplo, podem ser simulados de forma realista muitos tipos de gráficos e acabamentos especiais. Existe ainda a possibilidade de visualizar o produto sob diferentes condições de iluminação.

Quando um desenho se aproxima da fase final de produção, contudo, é essencial realizar um protótipo. Obviamente, este pode ser feito manualmente. Mas, para criar um protótipo realista, é muito mais aconselhável utilizar uma impressora de prova para imprimir os gráficos no material pretendido e uma mesa de corte e vinco digital para produzir uma maqueta exacta.

As mesas de corte apresentam vários tamanhos e uma vasta gama de possibilidades. Alguns modelos estão até preparados para realizar pequenos ciclos de produção.

造形パッケージングデザイン

パッケージデザイン技術は、近年大きな進歩を遂げました。特にデジタル技術における進歩が、パッケージのデザインと製造工程に大きな影響をおよぼしています。このシリーズは、パッケージのデザインにおける最新の技術を紹介し、これらの技術の進歩の恩恵を読者にもたらすことを目的に出版されました。デザインの作成と開発は、最新の3Dデザインおよび検査用ソフトウエアを使用して行われました。また、テンプレートは、デジタル制御のカット台で切断および折り曲げを行ったあと組み立てられました。このプロセスにより、デザインの精度が保証されるうえ、機能性と拡張性を備えたデザインが可能になりました。ただし、パッケージを設計する場合、使用する素材の厚さを考慮しなければなりません。寸法や素材の変更にともなうデザインの調整を行ってください。

パッケージ規格

世界中のいくつかの機構が造形パッケージのデザインのために業界規格を設けています。最も広く使用されているのは、FEFCO (European Federation of Corrugated Board Manufacturers) およびESBO (European Solid Board Organization) によって共同で確立された設計コードと、PPC (American Paperboard Packaging Council) により定義されている種別の特性です。

素材

パッケージのデザインと製造では、繊維素材を以下のように区別します。
紙：225 gsm（1平方メートルあたりのグラム数）未満の重さがある素材。
板紙：225 gsm以上の重さがある紙素材。
ボール紙：重さ150〜600 gsmの硬質素材。紙より堅くコーティングされているものもあります。

段ボール：紙や板紙の上または間に波形の紙素材の中芯（フルート）が接着されたもの。最も一般的な段ボールには以下4種類があります。

片面段ボール：波形の中芯にその中芯を保持するためのライナーと呼ばれる原紙を一枚張り合わせたもの。

両面段ボール：ライナー二枚の間に波形の中芯を一枚張り合わせたもの。

複両面段ボール：ライナー三枚の間にそれぞれ波形の中芯を二枚張り合わせたもの。

複々両面段ボール：ライナー四枚の間にそれぞれ波形の中芯を三枚張り合わせたもの。

素材と層の数に加えて、段ボールは波形の中芯の種類によっても区分されます。中芯のタイプは一般に、メートル（またはフィート）あたりの波形の数と中芯の厚さによりレターコードで分類されています。

本書では、次の三種類の素材をプロトタイプ（試作品）に使用しました。350 gsmの段ボール、1 mmのGフルート（薄型）段ボール、および1.5 mmのEフルート段ボール。また、「**基本パッケージング**」のFEFCO標準のデザインにおいては、立体イメージのシミュレーションに3 mmのBフルート段ボールを想定しました。

技術的考慮事項

板紙などに折り目をつける場合、折り目は折の外側（つまり山側）に付けます。しかし、段ボールの折り目（または、切り込み線）は折り目の内部に付けます。

多くの場合、素材の「きめ」（段ボールの場合は波形の中芯）の方向がデザインにとって重要です。きめや中芯の方向はパッケージの折りの仕上がりや構造上の安定性に影響します。デザイン作業にあたって、素材供給会社やメーカーとこの点を話し合うことをお勧めします。

印刷と仕上げの種類と品質を考える場合、使用する素材の表面を考慮することが重要です。例えば、表面が粗い素材は、細かいハイコントラストのグラフィックスには適しません。オフセット印刷、箔押加工、エンボス加工などには、コーティングされた高品質の板紙または段ボールが適しています。

パッケージ寸法

パッケージデザインで最も重要な点は、もちろんパッケージされる製品の寸法です。しかし、保護目的のパッキングやライナーのための空間、パッケージ外寸、パッケージの積み重ねまたはパレット上での積み具合、生産時に発生する素材の無駄、生産速度などの追加要件もデザインする際に考慮する必要があります。

パッケージデザイン

他の造形デザインと同様、今日のほとんどのパッケージデザインにはCAD（コンピュータ支援設計）プログラムが使用されます。

プログラムには、基本構造作成のための簡単なソフトウェアから、完全に生産過程を管理する非常に高度なアプリケーションもあります。

EskoArtworkはパッケージデザインソフト開発のグローバルリーダー的企業で、EskoArtworkのArtiosCADソフトウェアは長い間この業界で使用されています。この最先端のプログラムはプロの製造環境におけるパッケージデザインの完璧なソリューションといえます。しかし、すべてのArtiosCADの機能を必要としない、グラフィックデザイナー、パッケージデザイナー、および製品デザイナーのためのより手頃なツールとして、Adobe Illustrator®やPhotoshop®などのプログラムで使用できる様々なプラグインがEskoから提供されています。この本のデザインはすべて、これらのプラグインを使用して作成されました。また、これらソフトウェアのデモ版は付録のCDに収められています。

プロトタイプ

優れたソフトウェアプログラムにより、デザインの徹底的な検査が容易になり、手動によるテストの必要性が低減します。例えば、EskoArtworkのVisualizerプラグインを使って、様々なグラフィックスや特殊仕上げをリアルにシミュレートできます。異なった照明条件下でパッケージの仕上がりを仮想で事前に確認することも可能です。

しかし、デザインの最終的な生産段階では、プロトタイプの作成が不可欠です。もちろん、手作業でこれを作ることも可能ですが、校正プリンターを使用して対象となる素材にグラフィックスを印刷し、デジタル制御されたカット台と折り台を使用すると正確な実物模型を作成でき、よりリアルなプロトタイプが出来上がります。

カット台は様々なサイズと機能で選ぶことができます。小規模な制作工程での作成に適したモデルも販売されています。

结构包装设计

由于数字化功能的不断发展，近年来包装设计技术在设计和制造方面取得了巨大的进步。本系列丛书的内容使用最新技术制作，旨在为读者带来这些技术革新的好处。我们使用了最新的3-D绘图和测试软件创建和开发所有设计，并使用数字驱动裁床切割原型模板和制作折痕。所有这些工作意味着可以保证设计的精确度；设计具备应有功能并且可充分缩放。但请记住，在设计任何包装时必须考虑所使用材料的厚度。如果更改尺寸或使用其他材料，很可能需要调整设计。

包装标准

许多全球性组织发布了多个用于结构包装设计的行业标准。其中使用最广泛的是FEFCO (European Federation of Corrugated Board Manufacturers, 欧洲瓦楞纸板制造商联合会)和ESBO (European Solid Board Organization, 欧洲硬纸板组织)联合确立的设计准则以及 PPC (American Paperboard Packaging Council, 美国纸板包装协会)规定的分类样式特征。

材料

在包装设计和制造中，以下纤维材料类型之间存在区别：
纸张： 重量小于 225 gsm (克/平方米)的材料
纸板： 重量大于 225 gsm 的实心材料
硬纸板： 重量介于 150 和 600 gsm 之间的实心材料；比纸张更坚硬，通常涂有涂层
瓦楞纸板： 胶粘在纸张或纸板上或之间的楞纸。最常用的瓦楞纸板包括：

单面： 一层瓦楞纸粘在一层纸张或纸板上

双面或单瓦： 一层瓦楞纸粘在两层纸张或纸板上

双瓦： 两层瓦楞纸粘在三层纸张或纸板上

三瓦： 三层瓦楞纸粘在四层纸张或纸板上

"除了材料和层数，瓦楞纸板还可以通过楞形来描述。楞形通常使用字母代码表示，并由每米/英尺内的楞形数量和楞形厚度决定。

本书中的原型使用三种材料：350gsm 硬纸板，1mm G楞瓦楞纸板，1.5mm E楞瓦楞纸板，3mm B楞瓦楞纸板。

技术注意事项

在硬纸板中折叠折痕时, 折痕应在计划折线外, 即折叠从折痕开始。但是, 对于瓦楞纸板中的折叠, 折痕 (或刻痕) 应在折线内。

在许多情况下, 材料纹理的方向 — 或瓦楞纸板中楞形的方向 — 很重要。纹理/楞形可以影响折痕的质量以及包装的总体稳定性。完成设计前, 最好与材料供应商和制造商讨论这一点。

选择印刷和整饰的类型和质量时, 所用材料的表面是一个值得注意的重要问题。例如, 粗糙的纸板不适合精细或高对比度图案, 而高质量纸板或瓦楞纸板 (具有至少一个光滑涂层面) 则允许高标准胶印、箔冲压、压印等处理。

包装尺寸

设计包装时, 最重要的注意事项当然是要包装产品的尺寸。但是也要注意一些其他问题, 例如为缓冲层或衬垫留出空间, 包装的外部尺寸, 如何堆放和/或放入货盘中, 生产期间的材料浪费, 以及生产速度。

包装设计

和大部分其他结构设计形式一样, 现在的大部分包装设计使用 CAD (计算机辅助设计) 程序完成。CAD 具有许多类型, 从允许您创建基本结构的简单软件, 到可以管理整个生产流程的高度先进的应用程序。

EskoArtwork 是开发包装设计软件的世界领先厂商。他们的 ArtiosCAD 软件已经在业内使用了数十年。这款先进的程序为专业制造环境中的包装设计提供一套完整的解决方案。但对于不需要 ArtiosCAD 的完整功能的图案、包装和产品设计人员来说, Esko 软件对 Adobe Illustrator® 和 Photoshop® 等程序的软件插件也是极为出色和更加经济的替代选择。本丛书中的所有设计均使用这些插件创建, 附带的 CD 中提供该软件的演示版。

原型

优秀的软件程序方便彻底检查设计并有助于减少物理测试的需求。例如在 EskoArtwork 的 Visualizer 插件中, 可以实际模拟许多图案和特殊修饰, 甚至可以在不同照明条件下可视化产品。

但在设计接近最后生产阶段时, 重要的是制作原型。当然可以手工制作原型。但使用打样打印机在预期材料上打印图案, 并在数字驱动的裁剪折痕床制作精确的实物模型是比制作实际原型好得多的方法。

裁床具有多种大小和丰富的功能。一些型号甚至适合小型生产过程输出。

α: Glue Flap Taper (usually 10° to 15°)

β: Secondary Dust Flap Taper (usually 15°)

γ: Primary Dust Flap Taper (usually 45°)

R, r: Tuck Flap Radius

Setback and Shoulder depend on board caliper and carton size

Panel Names and Terminology   **29**

	EN	DE	FR	ES
	Panel Names and Terminology	Seitenbezeichnungen und Terminologie	Noms des panneaux et terminologie	Nombre de los paneles y terminología
L	Length	Länge	Longueur	Longitud
W	Width	Breite	Largeur	Anchura
D	Depth	Tiefe	Profondeur	Profundidad
	Upper Tuck Flap	obere Einstecklasche	Pan rabattable supérieur	Solapa de cierre superior
	Lower Tuck Flap	untere Einstecklasche	Pan rabattable inférieur	Solapa de cierre inferior
	Top Closure Panel	obere Verschlussklappe	Panneau de fermeture supérieur	Panel de cierre superior
	Bottom Closure Panel	untere Verschluss-klappe	Panneau de fermeture inférieur	Panel de cierre inferior
	Dust Flap	Staublasche	Pan de retenue	Solapa de protección
	Glue Flap	Klebelasche	Pan encollé	Solapa de pegado
	Rear Panel	Rückwand	Panneau arrière	Panel posterior
	Front Panel	Vorderwand	Panneau avant	Panel anterior
	Left Side Panel	linke Seitenwand	Panneau latéral gauche	Panel izquierdo
	Right Side Panel	rechte Seitenwand	Panneau latéral droit	Panel derecho
	Shoulder	Kantenzugabe	Épaulement	Reborde
	Setback	Versatz	Décrochement	Distancia de sepa-ración
α	Glue Flap Taper (usu-ally 10° to 15°)	Klebelaschen-Anschrä-gung (meist 10°-15°)	Pan encollé biseauté (généralement, 10° à 15°)	Cuña de la solapa de pegado (en general de 10° a 15°)
β	Secondary Dust Flap Taper (usually 15°)	zweite Klebelaschen-Anschrägung (meist 10°-15°)	Pan de retenue biseauté secondaire (généralement 15°)	Cuña de la solapa de protección secundaria (en general 15°)
γ	Primary Dust Flap Taper (usually 45°)	erste Staublaschen-Anschrägung (meist 45°)	Pan de retenue biseauté principal (généralement 45°)	Cuña de la solapa de protección principal (en general 45°)
R, r	Tuck Flap Radius	Einstecklaschen-Eckradius	Rayon de pan rabat-table	Radio de la solapa de cierre
	Setback and Shoulder depend on board cali-per and carton size	Versatz und Kanten-zugabe abhängig von Materialstärke und Seitenmaßen	Le décrochement et l'épaulement dépen-dent de l'épaisseur et de la taille du carton	La distancia de separación y el reborde dependen del calibre y el tamaño del cartón

	IT	PT	JP	CH
	Nomi e terminologia del pannello	Nomes dos painéis e terminologia	各パネル名と用語	面板名称和术语
L	Lunghezza	Comprimento	長さ	长度
W	Larghezza	Largura	幅	宽度
D	Profondità	Altura	奥行き	高度
	Risvolto piega superiore	Aba de encaixe superior	上部差し込みフラップ	上褶边
	Risvolto piega inferiore	Aba de encaixe inferior	下部差し込みフラップ	下褶边
	Pannello chiusura superiore	Painel de fecho superior	上閉じパネル	上挡板
	Pannello chiusura inferiore	Painel de fecho inferior	下閉じパネル	下挡板
	Risvolto antipolvere	Aba anti-pó	ダストフラップ	防尘襟片
	Risvolto colla	Aba de colagem	糊代	胶粘襟片
	Pannello posteriore	Painel traseiro	後パネル	后面板
	Pannello anteriore	Painel frontal	前パネル	前面板
	Pannello lato sinistro	Painel lateral esquerdo	左パネル	左面板
	Pannello lato destro	Painel lateral direito	右パネル	右面板
	Spalla	Ombro	肩	肩
	Rientranza	Folga	逃げ	缩进
α	Conicità risvolto colla (in genere da 10° a 15°)	Bisel da aba de colagem (normalmente 10° a 15°)	糊代テーパー (通常10°〜15°)	胶粘襟片锥度 (通常10°至15°)
β	Conicità risvolto antipolvere secondario (in genere 15°)	Bisel da aba anti-pó secundária (normalmente 15°)	ダストフラップ二次テーパー (通常15°)	辅助防尘襟片锥度 (通常15°)
γ	Conicità risvolto antipolvere primario (in genere 45°)	Bisel da aba anti-pó principal (normalmente 45°)	ダストフラップ一次テーパー (通常45°)	主要防尘襟片锥度 (通常45°)
R, r	Raggio risvolto piega	Raio da aba de encaixe	差し込みフラップ丸半径	褶边半径
	La rientranza e la spalla dipendono dallo spessore e dal formato del cartone	As folgas e ombros dependem do calibre e do tamanho do cartão	逃げと肩の寸法はカリパスとカートンのサイズによります。	缩进和肩取决于纸板大小

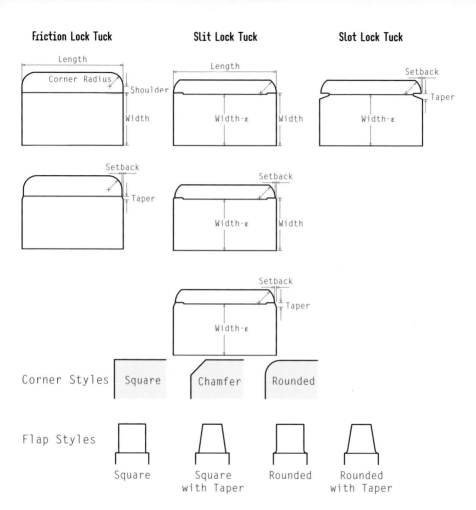

EN	DE	FR	ES	IT	PT	JP	CH
Lock Tuck, Corner and Flap Styles	Typen von Einstecklaschen, Ecken und Laschen	Types de pan de fermeture, de coins et de rabats	Tipos de cierres, cantos y solapas	Stili di piega blocco, angolo e risvolto	Estilos de fecho, cantos e abas	ロック、差し込み、コーナー、フラップの形状	锁扣褶边、角和襟样式
Friction Lock Tuck	Einstecklasche mit Reibungs- arretierung	Pan à montage par friction	Cierre deslizante	Piega blocco a frizione	Aba de fecho por fricção	差し込みフラップ	摩擦锁扣褶边
Slit Lock Tuck	Einstecklasche mit Schlitz- arretierung	Pan à encoches de fermeture	Cierre ajustable	Piega blocco a fenditura	Aba de fecho por ranhura	切れ込み付き差し込みフラップ	切口锁扣褶边
Slot Lock Tuck	Einstecklasche mit Kerbarre- tierung	Pan à fentes de fermeture	Cierre con ranuras	Piega blocco a fessura	Aba de fecho por fissura	溝付き差し込みフラップ	槽口锁扣褶边
Length	Länge	Longueur	Longitud	Lunghezza	Comprimento	長さ	长度
Width	Breite	Largeur	Anchura	Larghezza	Largura	幅	宽度
Corner Radius	Eckradius	Rayon du coin	Radio del canto	Raggio angolo	Raio do canto	コーナー半径	角半径
Shoulder	Kantenzugabe	Épaulement	Reborde	Spalla	Ombro	肩	肩
Setback	Versatz	Décroche- ment	Distancia de separa- ción	Rientranza	Folga	逃げ	缩进
Taper	Anschrägung	Biseau	Bisel	Conicità	Bisel	テーパー	锥度
Corner Styles	Ecktypen	Types de coins	Tipos de cantos	Stili angolo	Tipos de canto	コーナー形状	角样式
Square	rechteckig	Carré	Cuadrado	Quadrato	Quadrado	角	直角
Chamfer	abgeschrägt	Chanfreiné	Biselado	Smussato	Chanfro	面取り	削角
Rounded	abgerundet	Arrondi	Redondo	Arrotondato	Redondo	丸	圆角
Flap Styles	Laschentypen	Types de rabats	Tipos de solapas	Stili risvolto	Tipos de aba	フラップ形状	襟样式
Square	rechteckig	Carré	Cuadrada	Quadrato	Quadrada	角	方形
Square with Taper	trapezförmig, angeschrägt	Carré avec biseau	Cuadrada en forma de cuña	Quadrato con coni- cità	Quadrada com bisel	テーパー付き角	梯形
Rounded	rechteckig, abgerundet	Arrondi	Redonda	Arrotondato	Redonda	丸	带圆角方形
Rounded with Taper	trapezförmig, abgerundet	Arrondi avec biseau	Redonda en forma de cuña	Arroton- dato con conicità	Redonda com bisel	テーパー付き丸	带圆角梯形

Friction Lock Tuck Dust Flaps   Slit Lock Tuck Dust Flaps

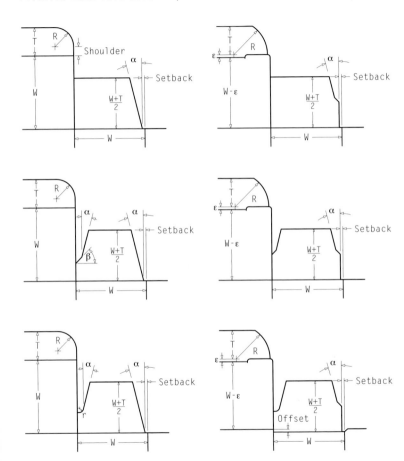

EN	DE	FR	ES	IT	PT	JP	CH
Dust Flap Styles	Staublaschentypen	Types de pans de retenue	Solapas de protección	Stili risvolto antipolvere	Estilos de abas anti-pó	ダストフラップ形状	防尘襟片样式
Friction Lock Tuck Dust Flaps	Einstecklasche mit Reibungsarretierung	Pan à montage par friction	Solapas con cierre deslizante	Piega blocco a frizione	Aba de fecho por fricção	差し込みフラップのダストフラップ	摩擦锁扣褶边
Slit Lock Tuck Dust Flaps	Einstecklasche mit Schlitz-arretierung	Pan à encoches de fermeture	Solapas con cierre ajustable	Piega blocco a fenditura	Aba de fecho por ranhura	切れ込み付き差し込みフラップのダストフラップ	切口锁扣褶边
Shoulder	Kantenzugabe	Épaulement	Reborde	Spalla	Ombro	肩	肩
Setback	Versatz	Décrochement	Distancia de separación	Rientranza	Folga	逃げ	缩进
Offset	Versatz	Décalage	Distancia de separación	Rientranza	Folga	オフセット	偏差

perforation knife

die-cut

scoring rule

EN	DE	FR	ES	IT	PT	JP	CH
Cutting, scoring and perforation die-mould	Schneide-, Rill- und Perfo-rations-Stanzwerk-zeug	Matrice de découpage, de rainage et de perforation	Molde de corte, hendido y perforación	Forma per fustel-latura, cordonatura e perfora-tura	Molde para corte, marcação e perfuração	カッティング、スコアリング、パーフォレーション ダイモールド	包装用的剪切, 刻线与穿孔冲模
perforation knife for zip	Perforier-messer für Aufreißla-schen	lame de perforation pour dis-positif de fermeture	cuchilla de perforación para el cierre	perforatore per strappo	lâmina de perfuração para o fecho	ジッパー用 パーフォレーション ナイフ	拉链穿孔刀
die-cut	Stanzmesser	outil de découpage à l'importe-pièce	troquelado	bordo	corte	ダイカット	冲切
scoring rule	Rillmesser	outil de rainage	regla de hendido	cordonatore	régua de marcação	スコアリング ルール	刻线尺

Regular Boxes

Square Tuck-lock Mailer

Side Panel Tuck Lock with Tabs

Side Panel Tuck Lock with Tabs

Thumb Locking Tab

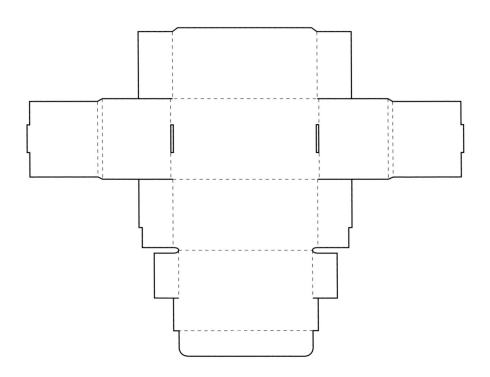

Tuck Lock Top with Half Dust Flaps

Side Panel Locking Tabs

Side Panel Locking Tabs

Tuck Lock with Dust Flaps

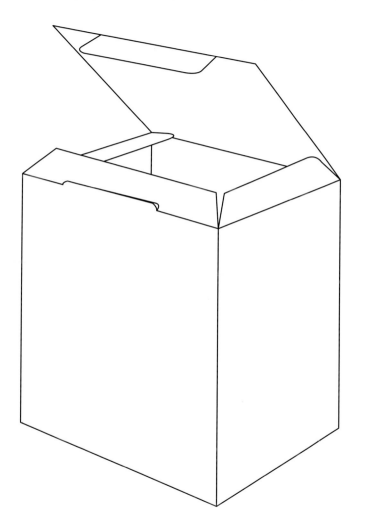

Tuck Lock with Dust Flaps

Reinforced Sides with Hinged Top

Reinforced Sides with Hinged Top **57**

Gusseted Interlocking Dust Flaps

Gusseted Interlocking Dust Flaps

60   Tuck Lock with Thumb Hole

Tuck Lock with Thumb Hole   **61**

Reinforced Walls and Top

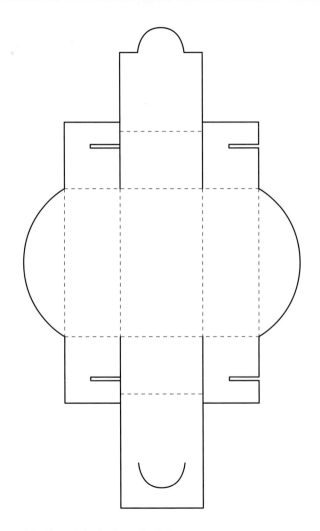

Top and Bottom Interlocking Dust Flaps

Top Panel Locking Tab

Reinforced Archive Box

Stackable Fruit Box

Stackable Fruit Box

Stackable Box

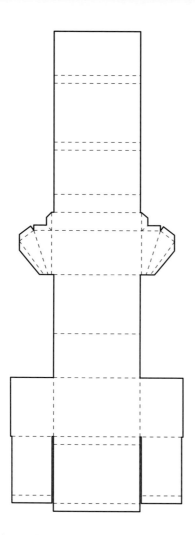

Reinforced Walls and Hinged Lid

Reinforced Double Tab Lock Box

Reinforced Double Tab Lock Box   **87**

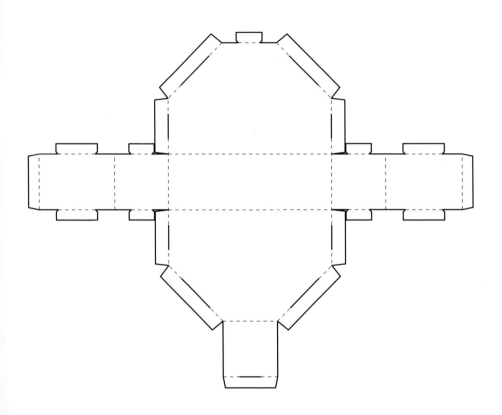

Irregular Hexagonal Tray with Locking Tabs

Irregular Hexagonal Tray with Locking Tabs

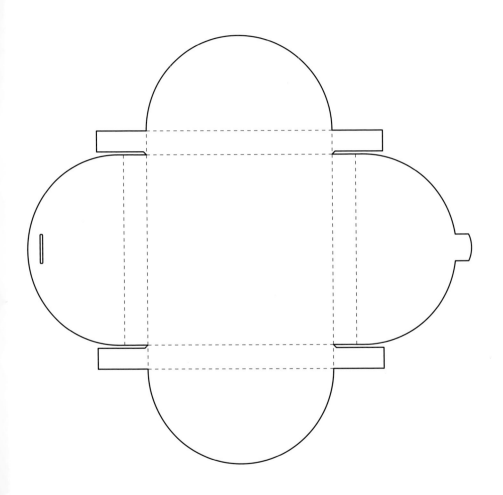

Half Circular Hinged Top Flaps

Display Packaging

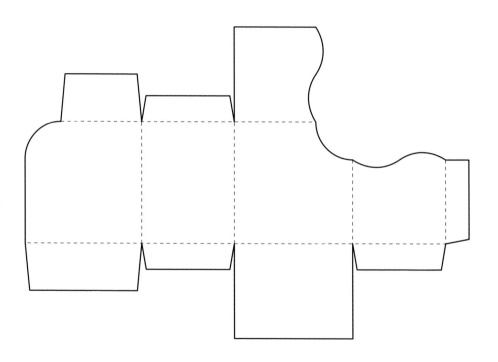

Sisplay Box with Open Corner

Sisplay Box with Open Corners   **97**

Twisted Display Box

Twisted Display Box

100   Fancy Hinged Lid

Front Panel Window, Triangular Sides

Octagonal Box with Window

Dispenser with Window

Dispenser with Window

Front Panel Window, Receding Top and Bottom

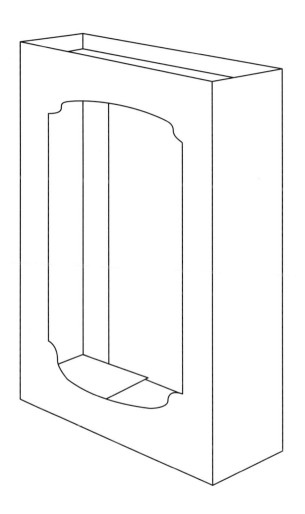

Front Panel Window, Receding Top and Bottom

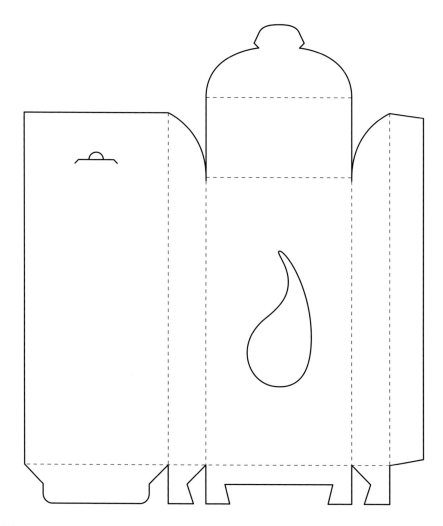

110   Front Panel Window, Rounded Top

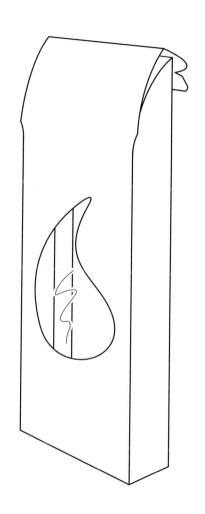

Front Panel Window, Rounded Top   **111**

Half Closed Tray with Viewing Hole

Half Closed Tray with Viewing Hole   **113**

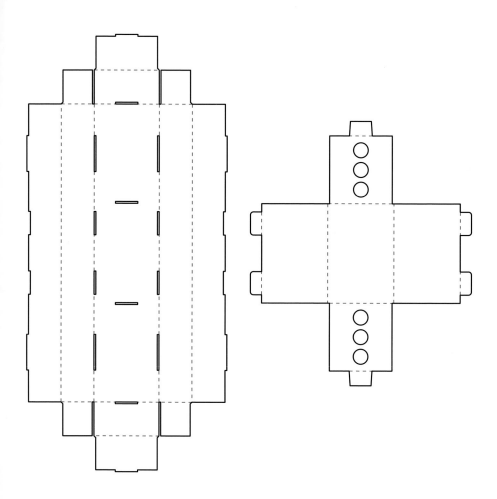

114   Display Box for Long Cylindrical Objects

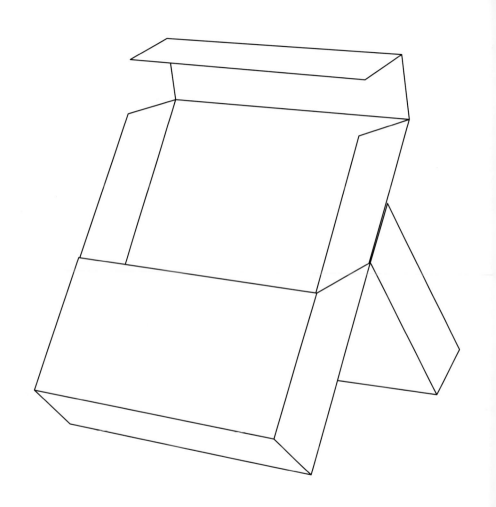

Display Box with Flip Top

Cube with Gusseted Corners

Cube with Gusseted Corners

120   Collapsible Cake Box

Display Box **127**

Display Box   **133**

134 Display Box

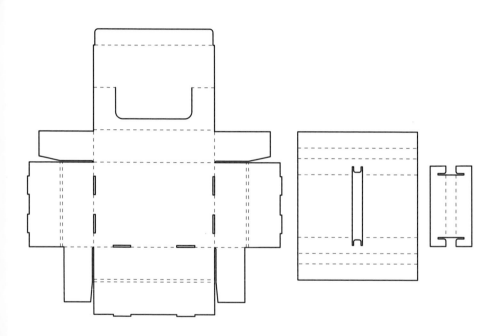

Reinforced Two Cell Display Box

Reinforced Two Cell Display Box **137**

144   Display Tray

Frame Support

Frame Support **147**

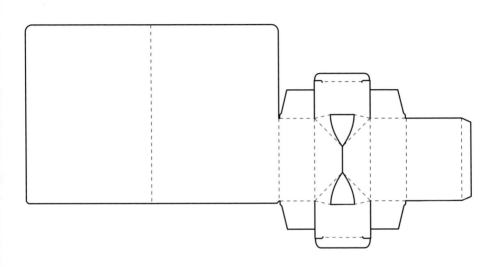

148   Display Box with Extended Back Panel

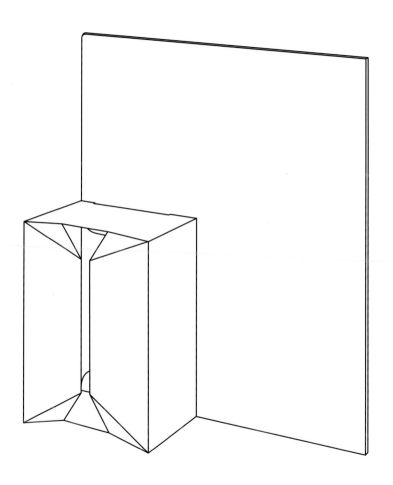

Display Box with Extended Back Panel   **149**

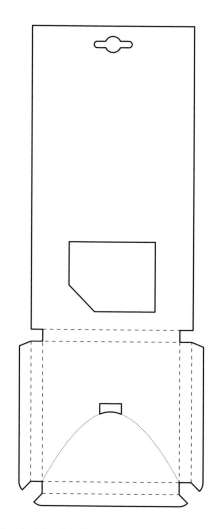

154   Hanging Perforated Display Box

Hanging Perforated Display Box **155**

Hanging Display Box with Edge Window

Hanging Display Box with Edge Window

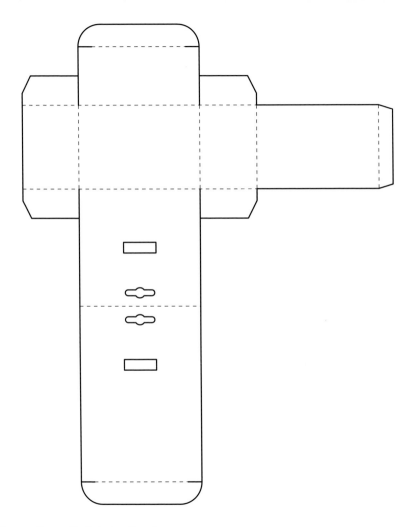

158   Box with Hanging Panel

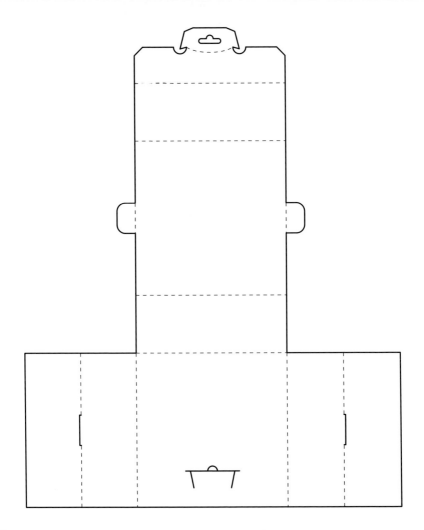

Tuck Lock with Hanging Hole

Tuck Lock with Hanging Hole   **161**

162

Hanging Box with Tapered Panels   **163**

Hanging Envelope

168   Box with Hanging and Locking Tabs

Perforation

Carrier

184 Presentation Box

Reclosable Trapeze Shaped

Reclosable Trapeze Shaped

Reclosable Trapeze Shaped

Cylindrical Tube

dispensers

Dispenser with Perforated Strips

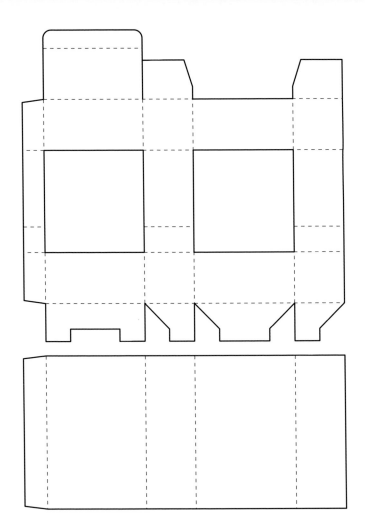

Dispenser with Double Window and Sleeve

Dispenser with Double Window and Sleeve   **213**

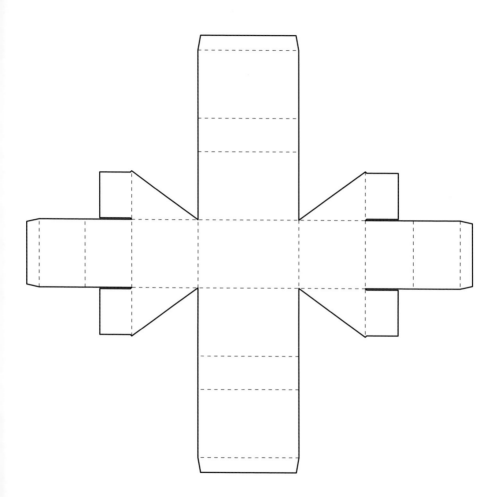

214   Dispenser with Two Hinged Closures

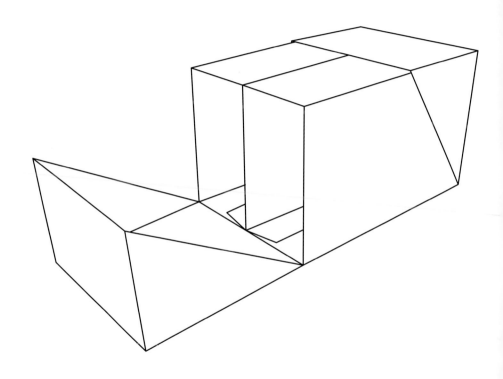

Dispenser with Two Hinged Closures   **215**

Dispenser with Sliding Lid

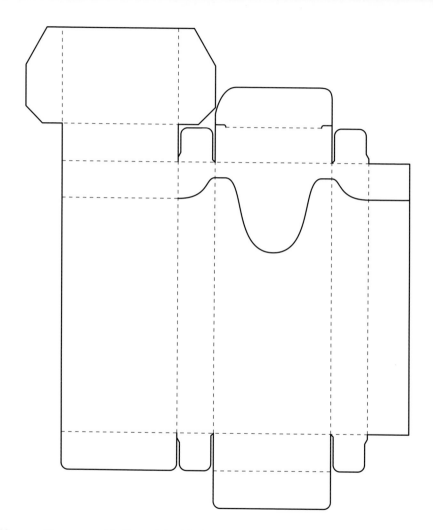

Dispenser with Special Double Lid

220   Dispenser with Sliding Lid

Supports and Dividers

Double Top Compartment

Double Top Compartment

Double Top Compartment

232   Central Divider

Ondulated Diagonal Divider

One-piece Four Cell Divider

One-piece Four Cell Divider

One Piece Six Cell Box

One Piece Six Cell Box **241**

Window Box with Central Support

Window Box with Central Support   **243**

244   Bottle Display Box

Bottle Display Box   **245**

Box with Circular Support Pads

Carrier with Additional Two Cell Divider

Carrier with Additional Two Cell Divider   **251**

Corner Support

Corner Support   **257**

Carriers

Pillow Pack Carrier

Bag-shaped Carrier

Bag-shaped Carrier

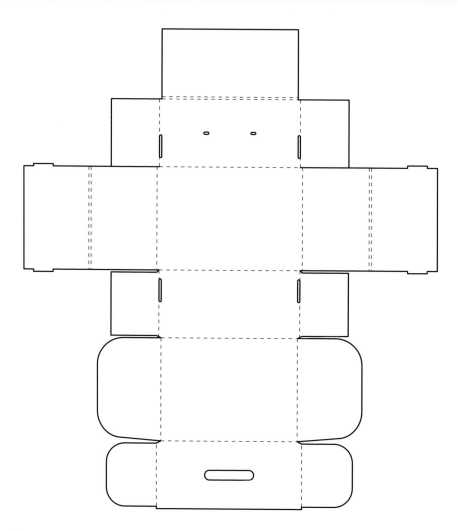

274　Reinforced Side Panel Carrier

House-shaped Carrier　　**279**

Rectangular Shaped Carrier

Tuck-in Side Slot Carrier   **283**

Bucket-shaped Carrier

292　Side Panel Handle Carrier

Side Panel Handle Carrier **293**

Heavy Object Carrier

Bottle and Can Holders

304 Six Cell Carrier

312 Four Cell Carrier

Bottle Holder

Bottle Holder

Can Carrier and Dispenser

330   Can Carrier

Can Carrier

Can Holder

338   Can Carrier

340   Can Holder

342　　Can Holder

344   Bucket Holder

348   Bucket Holder

350 Bucket Holder

Bucket Holder   **353**

Stackable Glass Tray   **355**

Special Shapes

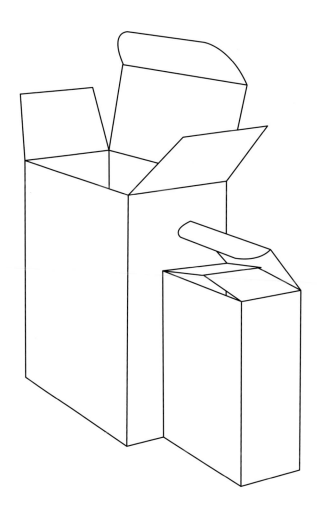

One Piece Double Package   **359**

Pillow Box with Thumb Hole

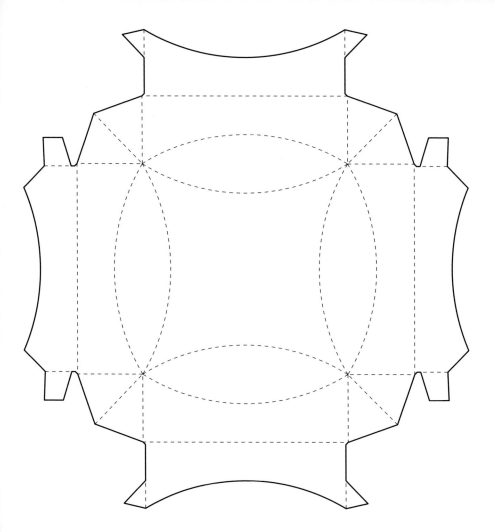

368   Box with Curved Tapered Edges

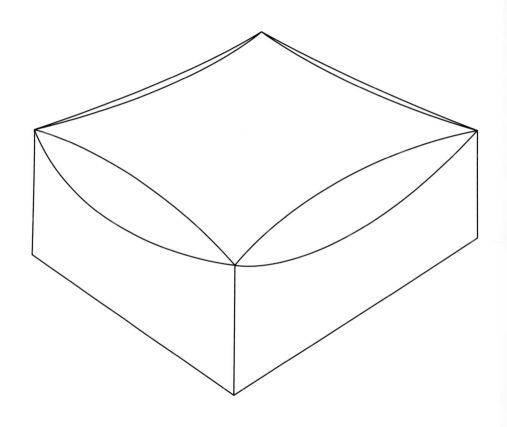

Box with Curved Tapered Edges

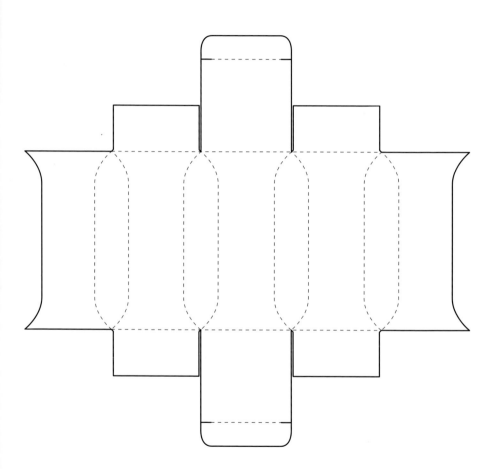

Box with Curved Tapered Edges

Box with Curved Tapered Edges   **371**

Soft Edge Box   **373**

Case with Rubber Band

Case with Rubber Band   **375**

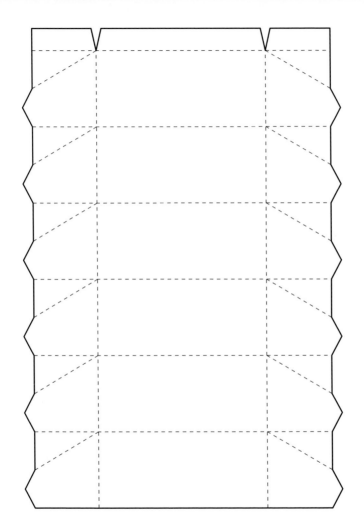

378   Octagonal Box with Lock Top and Bottom

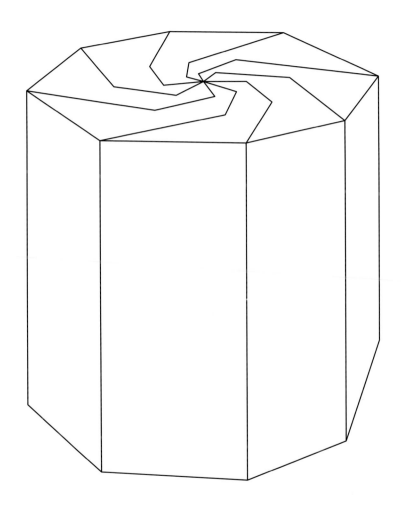

Octagonal Box with Lock Top and Bottom   **379**

Trapeze Based Box

386   Octahedronal Double Compartment

Octahedral Double Compartment   **387**

390   Fancy Box

396   Bottle Holder

Bottle Holder

Interlocking Triangular Double Box

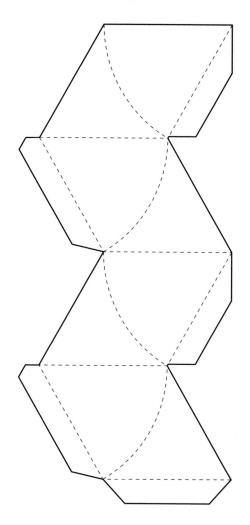

Octahedronal Box with Curved Edges

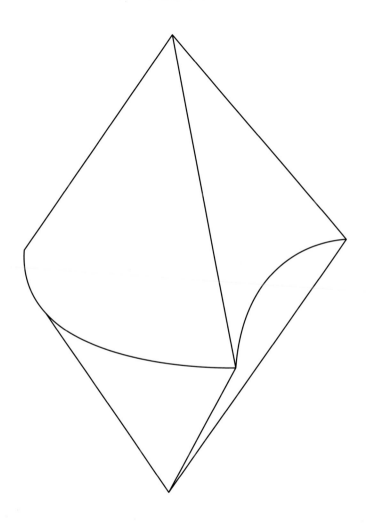

Octahedronal Box with Curved Edges

Irregular Octahedron

Cylindrical Box

Hexagonal Tapered Tube

Envelopes and Mailers

438   Envelope with Zipper and Locking Tab

Envelope with Zipper and Locking Tab 439

Envelope with Detachable Compartment   **445**

446   Video Tape Mailer

Video Tape Mailer   **447**

Envelope with Flexible Thickness

Flexible Self-seal Envelope

Flexible Self-seal Envelope

452   Tuck Lock Mailer

Self-sealing Mailer with Zipper

Self-sealing Mailer with Zipper   **455**

Book Mailer

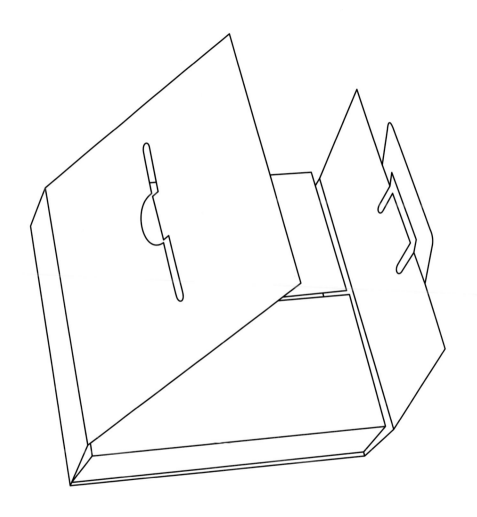

Book Mailer with Tuck Lock

466   Mailer with Double Locking Tab

Mailer with Double Locking Tab   **467**

Mailer with Locking Tabs

File Mailer   **473**

Gift and Letter Mailer

Flexible Length Poster Tube · **485**

Double Bottle Mailer

Double Bottle Mailer   **489**

Glass Mailer

492   Double-wall Mailer

Double-wall Mailer   **493**

Heavy Duty Mailer

Heavy Duty Mailer